Good

Good

Written by D. L. Watson

Illustrations by Kendra Watson

RESOURCE *Publications* · Eugene, Oregon

GOOD

Resource Publications
An Imprint of Wipf and Stock Publishers
199 W. 8th Ave., Suite 3
Eugene, OR 97401

www.wipfandstock.com

PAPERBACK ISBN: 978-1-7252-5778-8
HARDCOVER ISBN: 978-1-7252-5779-5
EBOOK ISBN: 978-1-7252-5780-1

Manufactured in the U.S.A.   02/20/20

Dedication

To our parents. Thank you for being good to us.

Do not be overcome by evil, but overcome evil with good.

—ROMANS 12:21

Contents

Preface

This book is not titled *Good* because I'm under the impression that its poems are particularly well written. It is titled *Good* because its poems focus on what is good in the world rather than on what is ambiguous or apathetic. I hope you will read these poems out loud, as they are intended to be read, and find them fun, thought-provoking, and good.

GOOD MORNING, GRACE EATER

Autobiography

Good Morning, Good Morning

Good morning, good morning, the sun has been born
To the eastern horizon, now blessed by the warm.
It's an age-old story, the epic of life —
The sun grows old in hiking the sky.

He marries the clouds and highlights her grace
While she softens the burning of his passion-filled face.
And their life lived together is a product divine
Where she makes him tender, and he makes her shine.

The world below looks up above
And renews its faith in the existence of love.
And for some time the people assume
Happily ever after for the clouds and her groom.

But the western horizon is too sweet a death
For the sun to argue his rightful time left.
With a final kiss, he paints his bride pink
While the whole world watches his radiance shrink.

The sunset brings tears because the clouds do not know
If the darkness that takes her will ever let go.
And so she is mourning, unseen in the night.
There's a glimmer in the distance, but she takes it as trite.

Her sadness consumes her until it breaks her resistance,
And she admits that she's tired of being part of existence.
But as soon as hope departs from the bride,
A slight illumination starts tickling her side.

And then the moon's face pronounces her form,
And the clouds acknowledge the husband's warm.
She begins to weep, but not in despair.
She weeps for the beauty suspended in air.

Her tears fall hard upon the estate
Of a feeble widow who stayed up late
To witness the moon consoling the clouds
With a message of peace through the thunderous shouts.

The widow prays nightly to the God of the moon,
"Thank you for the day, but deliver me soon."
Until when, one morning, there was no sun born,
For the mourning night clouds had emptied her storm.

The moonlight had pulled her, a traction so sweet,
Out of her sky, so cluttered with grief.
It supported her form with the most tender care
As she passed through the stars, her body laid bare.

Until, like a beggar who has had a king's feast,
The clouds felt fullness and looked to the east.
"Good morning, good morning," the sun told his bride,
And her form was made solid as she snuggled his side.

Until They Are Reality

I have the blessing of having a dream every night in which I die
And when I wake up to the light, I'm sprite and high from having life
I spring from bed like Scrooge on Christmas morning
And without warning, I run across the floor toward the door
I throw it open groping for the holy notion known as hope and
I run to the kitchen window, thrust it up and tuck my head inside
The tiny opening that shows the world outside
I see the serene scenery seeped in grimy bricks and glossy garbage
I see the rats rummaging, a cat stalking, a sky gray and growling
I see a fence rusting and a street bustling beyond the perimeter it draws
And even though I know the sight might imply a plight of blight
I'm excited by the light that wasn't there through the night
And how it seemed, in my dream, death had got a grip on me
And how I knew, when I woke, God had given me new hope
I don't want to die! I don't want to die!
Do I need a better reason to be glad to be alive?
Happy are the feet of he who makes the choice to run
While acknowledging walking would bottle up all his fun
Blessed is the man who can see he has a life
Because the implication made is that he's living in a light
I have this silly dream in which I die and leave the world
The dream is my gift, and that's all it is
A bit of grace that God has placed upon my stupid, stoic face
I wake and see my worst mistake would be to let it go to waste
And so I chant in grave reflection:
"Come upon me, Resurrection."
Because dreams are just mentality
Until they are reality
I heard the Son of God came here
They said he died and rose
I heard that story isn't true
And so existence goes
But in a world so *so* absurd and filled with stupid dumb
I take the hope that I can get and place my bet on love
And so I chant in this reflection:
"Come upon me, Resurrection."
Because dreams are just mentality

6

Until they are reality
So I chant in this reflection:
"Come upon me, Resurrection."
Because dreams are just mentality

Tangerine Trees

This morning, I woke up. It felt rather nice.
Kept inept while I slept — helped the sleep to suffice.
Reminisced with a fist rubbing sleep from my eyes
On the dream that had blessed my sleep through the night.

The previous night, I lay down to sleep.
My brain powered off. I was back on my feet
In a grove lined with clover and tangerine trees,
A citrus aroma composing the breeze.

Meandering forward, I thought of this place
As contrived by a mind to manifest grace —
The grassy green carpet, the warmth in the space,
The tangerine trees burning with praise.

How could this not be some product of will?
I breathed in the air 'till I'd taken my fill.
I lay in the clover, remained there until
My thoughts in that grove went from sluggish to still.

I fell asleep there and woke in my bed.
The tangerine trees still burned in my head.
"Father in Heaven, hallowed," I said.
I wanted more sleep. But I got up instead.

Momentary Infatuation

Here I sit so stupidly, surrounded by this coffee scene,
And there she goes to take the seat that's just beyond my laptop screen.
And now my mind is dumb debris, wafting in a mental sea
Of lovely thinking thoughtlessly confirming my humanity.
It's not the way I want to be — so easily, susceptibly
Succumbing to a desperate plea that grows now exponentially
With every moment in which she sustains her presence, flippantly,
Neglecting my new tendency to see not one iniquity,
But rather, with totality, regard her as morality
To guard her with a fervency from imposing impurity.
But as it is, unfortunately, I've killed the possibility
Of embracing the humility required for the ability
To engage this angel verbally with words that tell her truthfully
That when she sits so beautifully, she keeps all worry away from me.
Provided her proximity, peace is my reality.

People: Part 1

It's all about people.
And people agree.
But people like you
Aren't like people like me.

People like me
Say it's 1, 2, 3,
While people like you
Say it's A, B, C.

And people like you
And people like me
Aren't like people like them,
Cause people are free.

People believe
That people will see
The value endowed
In what people call "We."

But people live life
And people, indeed,
Become more like people
Who live for the "Me."

People get broken
And people proceed
To hating the people
Composing their breed.

People keep asking
How people should be,
Cause the question is hard,
Most people agree.

It isn't sufficient
To write out an answer —
If I write out a cure,
I haven't *cured* cancer.

But I point with my words
And hope people see —
It's all about people,
But not about "Me."

Something Important Like Corporate

The full-time office job necessitates habits and daily traditions
that work as steppingstones from one hour to the next.
There's a rhythm within which these habits and traditions occur
so that they bleed into one another and offer a slight challenge of efficiency,
and conquering the challenge feels much like perfecting a dance.

You begin with your laptop. It goes in the port.
You lift up the screen and turn on your work.
As it is loading, you take off your shoes,
go from sneakers to dress then continue to move
with your cup in your hand from your desk to the kitchen,
get you some coffee then return to the mission
of starting your day in smooth operation.
You open up email, you sip your libation
pretending the purpose within this routine
is something not worthless . . . you have to believe.
There's meaning in corporate.
These meetings contribute
to . . . something . . . important . . .
But it's really no use.

Beer

The beer begins
With beer, meet lips,
And trickles in
Like medicine.
The beer pretends
A reticence,
And, in a sense,
That's what it is —
A reticence,
Composed of its
Time-justified
Self-confidence.
Magnificent
In how it plows
My deficit
Of ebullience.
Splendiferous,
What more to say?
The beer begins
To end my day.
My God, my God,
Your splendor lives.
You gave me life.
Now I exist.
Now let me not
Neglect what is.
The beer begins
With beer, meet lips.

Comedy Central Presents

Is this fist a reminisce of his kiss you witnessed
When he pissed on your bliss like it's on his hitlist?
When you sit and admit that you're scared witless,
Is his lip at the tip of your fit-filled Asterix?

Remix these bits.

Can this hand reprimand a damned sham of a grand slam
When he slammed spam and ran like a sand-spurred ram?
When you stand and demand you're more than just ham,
Are you pissed just a bit you once said, "I am ham"?

You didn't have to say it, you didn't have to write it.
But you did have to fight it, and you fought it like a ham.
A cruel fate is a fool's fate.
The rule states it's your fate.
Your hate's late. It may be great,
But great hate's like a daybreak —
It should wake with haste at the start of the day
And make a grand entrance all like "Hip hop hooray!"
Not come alongside the dinner plate
Where ham's being served before saying grace.
Amazing grace, how sweet the sound,
You once were lost but now you're bound.
A round tubby piggy, an open-flame roast.
You plead with your eyes. Satan spits and says, "Gross."
You're done, tubby piggy, don't you dare call God hateful.
You married the Devil, and the Devil's unfaithful.

Remix these bits.

This just in: you're not dead.
Divorce the unfaithful and stomp on his head.
You do have to say it, it's helpful to write it,
But you don't have to fight it — wrath has been fed.
Why the hell do you keep getting into hell's bed?
Sit and reminisce on his fist in your lip
And the sick sense of bliss your wince provided.
Is this sick sense worth the roast to which you've been guided?

Now you scoff at the story, you laugh and you leave.
Your hate has passed through like Adam and Eve.
It's your morning of glory where you kiss him again.
You announce he's your lover, your mentor and friend.
You sigh at my story, but I will sigh most.
Goodbye, tubby piggy, I won't make the roast.

For Another

You are a matter of opinion
A selfish decision
A part of a system
By which I abide
A bridge to a schism
That hinders my living
I've based your existence
On your place in my mind

But now you are gone
You've travelled beyond
The fickle thought pattern
Under which you were drawn
And now in third person
I watch this get worse and
Disperse all these verses
To try and move on

But what a lost cause
No cause for this loss
Beyond what I thought
Was a justified pause
To process the matter
Of us and together
You clearly knew better
I clearly need God

And with that confession
I swallow my lesson
I pray for some grace
To slaughter my heart
To sever the tether
That caused me to follow it
Largely my sin but now
Hardly a part of me

God is the giver of grace
And I give him my praise

For the system he made
When he sent down a Savior
But here I am finding
Unfortunate timing
From which has resulted
A new desperation

You are a matter of fact
However I act, whatever I think
Your life is for God
You're totally free
And by that admission
I ask you the question
Of whether or not you would
Give grace to me

You are a palindrome
Beautiful either way
With or without me
You are great
Your spirit is sensitive
Damn the whole world
Were the world to degrade
Such a beautiful girl

That thought is the notion
Behind the commotion
Now consuming my thoughts
And fickle emotions
You don't fear reality
And yet your mentality
Maintains a purity
It radiates avidly

What purpose resides
In the designation of life
To defend what is pure
From ambivalent crimes
I'm a man in a world
That cannot decide

If God made it so
Or if man made up lies

And I fear what is not
A fear that I ought
To maintain, all the same
It's the fear that I've got
It's anxiety shaking
My mind in the making
The world might take you
My misery thought

But then, when I breathe
And find brief relief
I know I've let go
Of protecting her need
My right to protect her
Is less than conjecture
The best way to bless her
Is by letting her be

Zombie Creatures

I've got apathy surrounding me.
It's part of me. Undoubtedly, it's cowardly,
but how are we supposed to be
when most the world won't go to sleep
to close their eyes and have a dream?
I had a dream of living things,
not zombie creatures staggering.
It's flattering to think we're clean,
but we just gargled LISTERINE®.
It tastes pristine, but truth be told,
we've sprayed cologne upon our mold.
Zombie creatures exercise.
Zombie creatures use their eyes.
They have religion and they live by it.
Zombie creatures maintain a diet.
Zombie creatures do the things that indicate a beating heart.
But after they have done their things, zombie creatures fall apart.

A Tissue in Water

Like a tissue in water,
His body went rotten.
His pieces were worthless,
His whole was forgotten.

By absorbing the world,
He dissolved in the ocean.
His decay softly wafted
In jellyfish motion.

People: Part 2

It's all about people.
And people agree.
But people like you
Aren't like people like me.

To see a good action,
I have to assume
It's what the do-gooder
Intended to do.

But people like me
Say it's A, B, and C,
While your people agree
That it's X, Y, and Z.

So we get confused
When we're cut to the heart
To help a humanity
Falling apart.

Everyone's different,
So how should we know
What thing we ought say
Or which way we ought go?

The result is a stasis —
We find ourselves stuck
Attempting to fix
The belligerent muck

Proposed by thought patterns
Not crafted by truth
But by pieces the thinker
Extracted and skewed.

And after we're trapped,
We get jaded perspectives,
Which turn the world sour
And us ineffective.

Then all of a sudden,
There's a feeling inside
That accuses our joy
Of being a lie.

Then it's no longer easy
When we find ourselves caught
Between doing what's good
And doing what's not.

And we're trapped in this spiral
That's pulling us down.
We wanted to help them,
But we need help now.

I let out a whisper
Intending to shout.
Why am I here?
How do I get out?

The downward continues.
I'm drowning in dread,
Unable to see
That I'm stuck in my head.

I'm telling myself
That this life is despair.
I tried to do good,
But nobody cared.

Is it all about people?
I want to say so,
But when I look to the people,
They're telling me no.

Cross Borough

This bar eats people alive, I think.
Digests them with watery drink.
It attracts the loneliness off the street
And pretends to make it shrink.

I'm a first-time patron, but it's easy to see
The reality of this scene —
Shell-shocked children whose bodies
Dripped into adulthood. It's bleak.

Today emptiness came and went,
And yet here I sit, feeling spent.
I hold a newspaper.
I read a cartoon that I don't get.

I put it down and check my phone
For unexpected messages. Who knows?
I'm always hoping someone will argue
That I'm not alone.

But I am. And here there is no piano man
Or bartender named Sam.
There's just a guy filling glasses for sorry asses,
Which is what I am.

Beer became banal long ago.

I leave for home on my bike. It's subtle
How I weave through the streets
Sprinkled with leaves and clutter
And a man with no home, shoes, or rebuttal.

The sun setting whitewashes the grime
With shine, and I'm susceptible to its trick
Every time — I foolishly think it's nice.
But then the setting is night.

My ride suddenly feels unclear,
As if it had been on a track

But now I have to steer,
Because I am out of my element here.

This piece of the city has never come around me,

And now my foreign understanding
Of my unfortunate surrounding
Gives my mind the kind of grounding
Whose Gravity is fear.

There's a bitter hate in a voice that says,
"What do you want?! What do you want?!"
A gun gets pulled, held to a man's face,
And I'm like, Whoa. What is this place?

I don't wait for resolution. I move quick,
Feeling sick, feeling angry at all of it.
I weave the streets, cross the bridge,
Now back on track, back to being spent.

Back in Harlem. Back from my Bronx respite.

Back to the Basics

we ride on this train in hopes of avoiding
encounters that bring us that itch of annoying
by casting our vision to the floor or the ceiling
while plugging our ears we sit so coy and we
know this is simply the way of the world
no eye contact but i'll still check out girls
judgments flow freely from how i am feeling
insecurity leads me to hate what is more
is i recognize all of this it's not a surprise
to hear that this setting in front of my eyes
is a case of humanity butchered by humans
we keep on existing after we've died
i am rewinding my mind back to be
a bit happier healthier heartier see
i was better all over before all the closure
of fantasy fun and adventure i need
to go back to the basics of walking indeed
there is even a joy in just talking and we
should reclaim the significance cast the indifference
back to its bitter abyss and then leave

People: Part 3

It's all about people.
And people agree.
But people like you
Aren't like people like me.

It's all about people,
And I dare make the claim
That people hate people
Because we're the same.

People begin
By looking for friends
But end up looking
For means to an end.

Then people find value
In the people they know
Thinking, "Look at my people!
The places I'll go!"

Then some of our people
Get right in our way,
And our value for people
Starts slipping away.

And we live in this mode
Of mind disarray
In which people are cattle
In this game that we play.

And we think with our eyes
Because we haven't the faith
To believe in a truth
That could cripple our hate.

Our life is directed
By what we can see —
"I only hate people
That choose to hate me."

We go on this way
Feeling content,
Not being too twisted,
Just slightly bent.

Talk of redemption
And matters of faith
Become simpleton subjects,
Fallen from grace,

And suddenly we're trapped
In a ridiculous crate
That doesn't exist
Except for our hate.

And the ones that show up
To help us get out
Either damn or redeem us
With what they're about.

They say there's a God,
And that's just the start.
We turn subtle scoffing
Into an art.

Of course we reject them.
Not worth the fuss.
We only hate people
That choose to hate us.

Now it's back to the basics.
This method is dry.
It's all about people,
But we don't know why.

And on that thought,
Who is the "We"?
I assumed I had people,
But it's really just me.

Finally it clicks:
I feel so alone,
And the thing I need most
Is to feel like I'm known.

But there's no one around,
And there isn't a sound
Of potential companionship
Here on the ground.

Is it all about people?
I thought so, but why?
The stars overhead
Respond from the sky.

It's all about God,
But we get it wrong.
He gives us, his people,
A part in his song.

Written, intended,
Divinely inspired.
We love it as kids,
But then we get tired.

The song continues,
Oh what a friend.
The chorus has come.
It will come again.

People are precious.
They matter a lot.
But that thought alone
Can make the heart rot.

People have value,
But that's only because
God is the one
Who gives value to us.

He made us and gave us
His image to show
He cares for his people.
He wants us to know.

It's all about God,
And so I am free
To choose to love you
In the way he loves me.

It's all about God.
When will we agree?
The one who made you
Is the one who made me.

And the one who made you
Put those stars in the sky.
And the one who made me
Put these thoughts in my mind.

And the one who made us
Is the one who made them.
He loves us and wants us
To sing once again.

I'm Making a Point Here

Things aren't always black and white — there is a shade of gray.
And yet it is consistent — my heart breaks every day.
I see a stranger near me smile at a simple thing.
I pet a puppy's belly while he kicks in jubilee.

I eat a chocolate cupcake and I praise the baker's name.
I tell my friends, "I love you," and I hope they say the same.
I let my heart be warmed by cliché absurdities.
I ring a bell three times a day to give three angels wings.

I do my job and even though sometimes I must complain,
I ease the strain with gratitude for food upon my plate.
I write out silly poems with the hope that someone reads
A line that makes her giggle or a thought he sorely needs.

Things aren't always black and white — there is a shade of gray,
And I cannot account for the reality of pain.
But if my heart is broken for the people that I see,
I'm more inclined to help in faith they'll do the same for me.

I know that most the time they won't. But still I choose this way —
I make a point of making sure my heart breaks every day.

For One

You are a matter of timing
Like rhythm and rhyming
You keep undermining
The doubts I have made
I thought I was finding
A new silver lining
But you've been unwinding
The way I see grace

You're no consolation
Behind the formation
Of clouds that have darkened
My life with their rain
And you're not a libation
To wash it away
You're a payoff for patience
To translate my pain

Now I see it so clearly
God must love me dearly
I'd have to be dumb
To still wonder why
The ones who so nearly
Took me from you purely
Because I was lonely
Never felt right

So now I thank God
That His answer was not
A relenting nod
I now understand
Prior passions I'd caught
Were conceptual thoughts
But you hug my heart
When you're holding my hand

You were not what I saw
When I thought through it all

To anticipate what
I ought to expect
Thank God for my fault
What I saw was a doll
My creation was raw
And full of neglect

But then there you were
A dark pretty girl
With quiet demeanor
Lips eager to smile
Since then the whole world
Has become a bit blurred
Next to you as you burn
The dross of denial

And now in reality
My new mentality
Sees the insanity
I had assumed
Pretentiously thinking
My circumstance differed
I tasted the bitter
Before tasting you

Tasting this lesson
Is my new obsession
Your dark complexion
My praise-giving lips
Your skin is perfection
I kiss this confession:
No conceptual blessing
Could ever top this

Remember that moment
We each were alone
The moment before
You stepped in the shop
A bagel, a coffee
We've both always known

When good things are close
It's the blessing of God

And now we are finding
The point of this writing
The point of our binding
To highlight God's grace
I close my eyes tightly
To pray for God's guiding
He opens my eyes
And there is your face

Our love does not suffer
By giving another
The glory as plunder
That's backwards, in fact
God gives us the wonder
That makes our love thunder
He extrapolates joy
When we recognize that

So let us rejoice
In collaborative voice
That God made the choice
To set us as one
We just complied
My beautiful bride
Now on to new life
Our prologue is done

The Missus Misses My Blowfish Kisses

The missus misses my blowfish kisses . . .
We lean to kiss, then quickly I
Will part my lips in the blink of an eye.
And thus our kisses turn to blurs
Of my parted lips, sucking on hers.
Thus the infamous blowfish kiss.
Did Romeo and Juliet know such bliss?
And yet, I am baffled. She now insists,
"I do not wish thy blowfish kiss."
"But love," I weep, "thou art not true.
The blowfish kiss exists for you."
"I do not wish it," she does insist.
"I find it weird, and far from bliss."
"Alas," I cry, "I bid goodbye
To the blowfish kiss. Oh why, God, why?"
And so we go, without the blur,
The testament that I love her.
And over time, I do adjust
To the edict she had made a must.
But just this night, I lie to sleep
Upon the bed for her and me.
The missus turns to face my face
And blinks her eyes, requesting grace.
"My love," she whispers, "I am amiss.
I miss thy mystic blowfish kiss."
I turn away and sigh a breath,
For that testament was put to death.
Left with hollow hopes and wishes,
My missus misses my blowfish kisses.

Grace Eater

If I ever lose my sight and I cannot see the world
I will look inside myself and know you've brought me to your home
I will sit and listen closely to the silence under the noise
And I will know you as the canvas and foundation of my joy
And if I lose my hearing while I'm sitting in the darkness
I will breathe in the aroma of the flowers in your garden
I will call that sweet sensation a piece of grace I never knew
And I will know through that aroma that I am truly breathing you
And if I lose the capacity to know that sweet aroma
I will taste a single strawberry and understand I'm not alone
And if I eat a bitter fruit, I will not curse your name
For you make beauty blossom, but first you send the rain
And when I cease to taste or smell and cannot hear or see
I will take the hand of anyone and know you're here with me
And when I die I'll have no way of taking in your grace
But my soul will rest within your palm preserving it from waste
Until the time arrives in which our Lord comes back again
And He wakes me from my slumber and I get to live with Him
But as it is, I'm living this: a life not yet complete
So I thank you, Jesus Christ, for every morsel that I eat
For a time will come when all I know will fade out of my view
And there is no going back. There is only knowing you.

GOOD THOUGHT RHYTHM

Words on Words

Everything is Language

We are nothing more than the language of God
Who spoke us into being
And so when we look around in grateful laughter
Everything we're seeing
Is another word that he spoke
From the bird's tweet to the frog's croak
You look up and see the silent constellations
Bragging about something
We're way below
First in jubilation
Then in tribulation
Then in jubilation
And it's all God's words
Working together like a poem
To make a ball of stone
Inhabited by worms
And he spoke a word like gravity
To hold the ball together
His words they work together
Like birds of a feather

A Lyric, A Crumb

There's gravity, but, honestly, that force is the exception.
Balls of rock and gas float like crumbs throughout expanse.
Nothingness and space receive universal predilection.
Nothingness allows the crumbs within to do their dance.

How vast a space for a crumb like Earth to merit infestation.
Witness the whole universe yet miss us in a glance.
If God bit bread and Earth fell forth, could we call this a creation?
Nothingness, perhaps . . . but are these crumbs by chance?

There's rhyming, but that language is a bittersweet exception.
Timing acts as nothingness to crumbs in certain places.
The lyricist must reminisce before his grand selection.
The former lines are nothingness. The final lyric chases.

Good Thought Rhythm

I really have no interest in writing without rhyme;
There's value in such style, but the style isn't mine.
It's true you might grow weary when you read all of my writing,
But one percent of readership will find it quite exciting.
For those who don't, I wish to give a partial explanation —
It partially explains, but it's more a demonstration.
The exciting bit in rhythmic lit is not just what you read —
It's how closely you can follow tricky dance steps as I lead.

Each syllable provided is intended as a step,
And the more you read the beat I lead the better we both get.
The point becomes both less and more than pomp and vain pretension
When the rhythm of your thoughts becomes a bodily extension.
The way you read heptameter can make or break your flow
When at first you see heptameter but then you don't quite know.
So I ask you, my dear reader, to have faith when I say,
I'm the leader, not the meter, so please step with me this way.

At first you'll trip a little bit. You might for several tries,
But my vision sees a rhythm in what's written. Trust my eyes.
You might trip and say it's wrong because it goes against the flow,
But give it a minute and you'll admit it, all like "Whoa!"
You'll find it fun and want to go again to get it right.
Now get consumed in the plume of the funky mood. Come on, try it.
Rhythm, rhythm, everywhere, but hiding from our view.
I'll provide the verbiage, but the rest is up to you.

Hear the click, make it fit, you may need to repeat this —
These verbal pieces need some verbal adhesive to be cohesive.
Whatever you do, there is a substance and a style.
My substance is thought, because the topic makes me smile.
My style is rhythm within the pieces I write.
I try to make them good — that's my side in the fight.
That's the good thought rhythm, and it's not just for writing —
It is applicable to what you do to make the world exciting.

Like I said, I have no interest in writing without rhyme,
For I have so much to build in such a short amount of time.

For years I had no clue that I was up against the clock —
I had a little bit of rhythm, but primarily good thought.
Until my psyche's poet lit a flame of conviction,
Now I'm invested in the method of the good thought rhythm.
So until my time comes and I'm laid down to rest,
I will rhyme to the metronome inside of my chest.

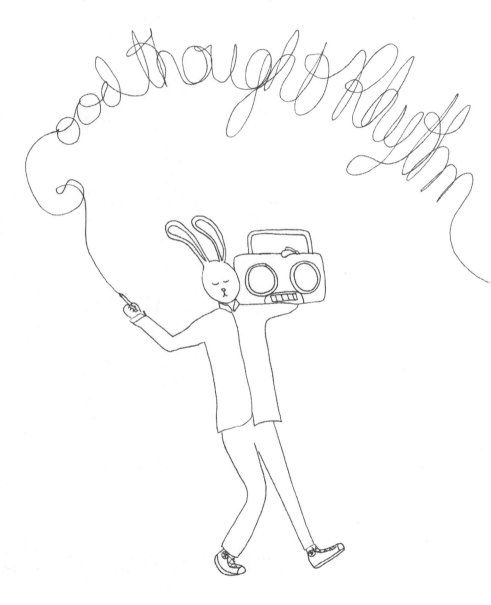

The Writing Game

I think a thought and like it,
so I write it, then I find it
is quite pleasing to my mind,
the source from which it came.
And I see this as a cycle —
a self-sustaining game.
It's entertainment for the poet
packed with anti-stoic statements
that are geared at subjects latent
like the truth in Plato's Cave.
These subjects are engrained
in the brain of he who thinks
in terms of philosophic notions
and in multi-colored inks.
These subjects are insane
to the simple and mundane
whose retention spans a solid inch
of that which people say.
They're lofty and abstract, perhaps,
and prone to be profound.
But logic is the endgame, see,
harmoniously sound.
A game sustained by its own play,
like food comes from the ground,
defining perfection as connection
moving around and around.
Insane, you say? Mundane you are.
Have yourself a candy bar,
and shut your mouth
and close your eyes.
This is food for thought.
You're looking for food for flies.
The writing game? It's just my thing.
Expression fit for a king.
Chuckling, I slap my knee,
as it is soliloquy.
And that's the dream, ain't it such?

Being happy without much.
I do that bit the best I can.
In a city of morale, I'm Superman.
I think a thought and like it,
so I write it, then I find it.
My only kryptonite is
a symbolic Leonidas
who fights my new ideas
on the back of both my eyelids
while I struggle in defiance
for a word that's in compliance
with my lyrical alliance.
But Leonidas dies
when I open up my eyes.
The word was right in front of me,
only in disguise.
And victory is sweet
when the enemy's your mind.
When you shatter self-made obstacles,
water turns to wine.
So here's a toast
to the writing game.
It's my method of finding
my way through the cave.
Try it out,
it's lots of fun.
But, spoiler alert,
God is the sun.
When you separate perception
from objective situation,
reality holds tried and true
on its firm foundation.
The writing game?
It's just my thing,
and you've every right
to disagree.
But process the question
before you leave —

is there a sun
that provides for our needs?
There's room for rebuttal,
I do understand.
I'm just not so eager
to discount a hand.
Is it a conflict in logic
or prideful resistance
that denies the statue
the sculptor's existence?
If there is no sun,
then why leave the cave?
You'd find no more truth
than if you had stayed.
And if the sun is not God,
then why care at all?
What joy's to be had
from a gaseous ball?
Humanistic triumph
is trite consolation
when juxtaposed with joy
without expiration.
Both are beliefs,
and both take faith.
But one is mundane
while the other is great.
I choose the latter,
and I'm not ashamed
to be labeled an idealist —
I'm self-proclaimed.
My God is ideal.
His son is the same.
My God felt the pain
when his son took the blame.
It's sickly profound
how keenly insane
are the thoughts that fester
in our hearts and brains.

Here is the son,
saying he's light,
and we shield our eyes
while saying, "Yeah, right."
And we did what we could
to blot out the sun,
for the sight was too bright
for the deeds we had done.
But such an attempt
was a juvenile display
of a child in a tantrum
not getting his way.
We kicked and we moaned
and we made ourselves cry,
but the writer of life
gets back up when He dies.
The sun arose and lit the sky.
By his light I saw my pride —
that symbolic Leonidas
on the back of both my eyelids.
Leonidas died
when I opened up my eyes
because the Word was
right in front of me
shining in the sky.
And humanistic triumph
is just fabricated life —
it's like praising Mona Lisa
for watching with her eyes.
A beautiful piece, I do agree,
but extolling a canvas is idiocy
when you neglect the due supremacy
of he who paints the imagery.
It's stupid to do
and makes you a fool
when you credit a house
to the work of a tool.
The way that I see it,

we've two distinct groups —
those who don't *want* to see the builder,
and those who do.
Again, I'm part of the latter,
and I'm not afraid
to take on the risk
that comes with a faith,
because you're taking a risk
no matter the camp
you pitch up a tent
or light up a lamp.
Yes, you're a faithful individual,
that I guarantee.
You just might not recognize
the way your faith intercedes.
You know next to nothing,
and the same applies to me,
and yet we operate like we're
precocious bee's knees.
I'm just wondering whether we're
whistle blowers at the scene,
neglecting perfection because
we don't want to see
a piece of potential
that could illuminate the key
that could open up the door
into a new mentality.
Just consider the metaphors
and the potential they provide
to show the reality
we keep missing in this life.
I think a thought and like it
so I write it then I find
the thought that I've written now has
a life apart from mine.
And even if the thought
that I ingeniously contrived
never understands that

it's a product of my mind,
I'm not finished, nor diminished;
my existence will survive.
My vision is sufficient
but the thought I wrote is blind.
Struggle and wrestle with
that metaphor for God,
the implications it proposes
and the changes it would cause.
Wrestle for some time
in your pursuit to understand
the lunacy involved
in the origin of man.
All theories are fuzzy
when they get to the how.
But the point is there is beauty
and you're living it now,
with the ability to rise
despite gravity pulling you down,
and with metaphors like eyes
to make the point that it's profound
that there's a hint of intention
that is objectively ground
within existence,
and it's consistent
how it works itself out.
Our eyes can see the beauty
that's supposed to be found.
Inside we feel the glory
of the beauty all around.
Surprised, we take a pen,
and then we lay it all down
into a lyric, then we hear it
and delight in the sound.
Thus creating new beauty
on which another can expound.
Thus shaking the stoic
out of his condescending frown.

Thus not feeling so bad
about not knowing every how.
Thus defining perfection
as connection moving around.
The writing game is saturated
with potential for glory.
These words were once alone
but now they're part of a story.
And that is humanity
if you'll open up your eyes —
a singular story
composed of multiple lives.
I think a thought and like it
because it's a child of my mind.
It's an existence that I find
has a nature subject to time.
But even when it dies,
I can resurrect it again
when I'm reminded by my kid,
"Father, this idea is a friend."
So I immortalize it with my pen,
ensuring it doesn't die again,
once an idea, now an end
to the beginning of the epic of men.
I think a thought and like it,
so I write it, then I find it
is quite pleasing to my mind,
the source from which it came.
And yet we always wonder
why God made us from the clay.
He spoke a thought and loved it
so he wrote it, then he noticed
it was starting to walk away,
the direction of the grave.
So he composed an immaculate thought
in which he superimposed his heart
so he could approach the other thoughts
in hopes of redirecting their ways.

He did it for the glory
of the perfectly written story
in which we get to share in the joy if we
would just accept his boy. But we
so often push away as if
we're seeking liberation.
We associate such faith
with judgmentalism and hatred,
completely neglecting our own hatred,
as if we're conveniently sanctioned
to hate upon the haters
as if our hatred will change them.
Now I don't know how our logic
became so undone,
but if you hate on the haters,
then the haters have won.
You'll be on the winning team,
so perhaps you'll find it fun,
but you're just strangling your teammates
until your own turn finally comes.
Of course, that entire issue is just
a tangent from the purpose
of expressing how human
triumph without God is
trite and worthless.
The writing game is fun
because it lets us be like God,
and if you take a minute to get in it,
that doesn't seem so odd.
Because the truth is if you use it
as a means to understand,
it's a self-sufficient justification
to the concept of God's plan,
meaning it begs the question
while giving the answer
all within the span
of the menial mental meanderings
of an otherwise mundane man.

You can use it as a tool
to take a teaching by the hand
and implement it as a brick
in the moral ground on which you stand.
For example, I give ample thought
and objective consideration
to the lines and rhymes
with which I give
this piece its population.
But it doesn't matter how hard I think
or meticulously I consider,
for clever rhythm never made
a bitter man not bitter.
What I'm saying here is there is very little
I can control when it comes to you,
because you're an autonomous human being,
and you're going to do things how you do.
The writing game has shown me this,
and so I give up any pursuit
that has me wasting precious energy
pushing a wall that I can't move.
So I channel that excess energy
into the doors that have potential
to be opened while I'm hoping
God might make me influential.
And that is why I'm standing here,
showing you this game,
asking you to ask yourself,
"Am I still in the cave?"
If you've yet to recognize the son
and the light he freely gives,
I ask you without malicious intent
to carefully consider this:
If we're in a cave and the sun is out,
the light we're going to see
is just a microscopic speckle
of the sun's intensity.
But if we leave the cave to see the sun

in all its splendid glory,
we no longer have the same kind of choice
or ease within ignoring.
We can lift our hands and try our best
to pretend there's nothing there,
but we're inevitably
still wretchedly and tragically aware,
wondering whether we're getting it wrong
with our hands in front of our eyes,
numbing ourselves to the prick of conviction
that spreads across the sky,
wasting precious energy
in avoiding the question of why
we can't just let our stupid hands
fall from our face down to our sides
and say, "The sun is pretty beautiful.
Thank God I came outside.
The cave in which I pitched my fit
was poisoning my mind."
And in that light, we might decide
it's right to just lie down,
and bask in all the beauty
as we lie there on the ground,
and marvel in the majesty
while considering the how
behind the overwhelming joy and peace
within this thought which we have found:
God is connection
moving around and around.
He spoke a thought and loved it.
We just happened to be the sound.

I Write As If

I know the Way to write within a rhythm
It starts with the ability to listen
I hear one's words until they make me antsy
And then
        I write
                those words
      as if
                they're dancing
I know the Way to write within a rhythm
And make it mine even though it isn't

The Bouncing Game

Have you ever played the bouncing game?

The bouncing game?

The bouncing game.

No, I've never played the bouncing game.

I'll show you how it's done.

Can you hear within your ear
the rhythmic beats our words create?

I think I do.

Then good for you —
that's how you play the bouncing game.

I think I see, but let me try.
I say some words, then what's my aim?

To hear the beat in what you speak.

And thus I've played the bouncing game.

Very good! And very clever.
You learn things fast, I have to say.
Would you like to play again?

We never stopped — the bouncing game!

Um, yes, but that isn't quite how it goes.
Allow me to explain.
You must take turns and give a chance —

I love the bouncing game!

Now listen here! That wasn't fair.
I don't wish to complain,
But it's rude to interrupt and you —

Will win this bouncing game!

But that isn't even how it works.

I'm sorry. I'm ashamed.

That's okay, just let me say —

The way to play the bouncing game?

. . .
Yes.
. . .

The bouncing game is more about
the thrill within the play,
and less about the winning.

        I think I get the bouncing game.

But see you're hogging all the fun.

        But the fun is in the play.

That is true but you keep taking
The final line —

        "The bouncing game"?

. . .
Yes.
. . .

        So?

So the fun is in the line.

        Is the line the only play?

You're treating it like competition.

        It's called the bouncing game.

It's played for fun.

        I'm having fun.

It's not as fun this way.

        I doubt that's true, you pouter, you.

Now just a sec —

        The bouncing game!

The competition's with yourself.

        Now that just sounds insane.

You're simply not enlightened.

        But I'm winning in this game.

I think I'm done. You have your fun.

        Don't walk away, that's lame.

I'll whisper out my victory:
I win this bouncing game.

Special Treatment

These artists are a special breed,
You have to meet them specially.
You can't just let them loose to scream
Away their lives and everything.
You have to meet them one degree
Above your heart's capacity
And feel what they have felt distinct
In your tongue and in your cheek.
These artists see a freedom clause,
Notarized with stamp and ink;
They shred the sheet then use their feet
To stomp the flaming garbage heap.
No policy they might admit,
No fallacy they can commit,
So long as they're creating.
All tethers they're escaping
To the best of their ability.
Look at their agility!
They idolize futility!
They're proud of their humility!
They'll sodomize your purity
And charge you for your charity.

You got a truth? They'll defy it.
Like zombies, artists love their diet.
You have to treat them specially,
This special, pure yet inbred breed.

They defy all things and mock all kings
And demand all puppets cut their strings.
They promise freedom to those who listen
Then lead their souls to pedant prison.
And then they say it's no big deal,
For unto them, God is not real.

These artists are a special breed.
You have to meet them specially.
Tongue-in-cheek humanity,
These artists are humanity.

With doubt as our new vanity,
Us artists question everything.

Fuh-fuh . . . faith

I took a turn to write a lyric
for all the deaf who wouldn't hear it,
and what I found was an empty frown
upon my face whose somber place
was grounded in a sharp distaste
for giving out a verbal grace
with no receptive body near it.

I took a pen and became a poet
for all the stubborn, weathered stoics.
But when I read my poetry,
they simply sat and stared at me,
and the beauty I put in every line
wafted away and was buried in time.

I painted a picture in order to find
some esthetic recognition on the part of the blind.
But much to my expectancy
the blind just sat expectantly
as I held my art before their eyes,
it broke my heart when none realized

I had placed a piece before their face
that lit the world with visual grace.
For they hadn't the means to receive the sight.
They could only dream about the sound of light.

And I was forced to admit against my proclivity
the lack of any real objectivity
involved in the concept of artistic dignity,
thus believing more heavily in relativity.

For how could I deny the truth behind,
"Beauty's in the beholder's eye."
The deaf couldn't feel it.
The blind had no idea.
From what I could tell,
objective beauty wasn't real,

and I only remorsed on this sobering thought
because its structure ran parallel to my understanding of God
in that spiritual substance seemingly ought
to be the reality that's manifested in art.

Only when it became too pressing
did I learn the value within this lesson:
the test is in guessing when's best to invest
in a method of resting when what you want most
is to run at full speed. Unless you undress
the finesse of the mess that has issued its creed
as an infiltrate seed, it will infiltrate you and grow like a weed.
Its mission is simple — to put deep within you
a kind of disease that feeds on your peace
and leads your two feet down a path of unrest.

Anxiety always, and dissatisfaction.
Depression compressed in a state of inaction.
The result is a fashion for leading a life
in which unoccupied time means something's not right.
What a sick, twisted plight, this method of madness
engrained in the human, whose action is badness.
Our actions are bad, we see it so clearly.
But passivity's worse. We believe it so dearly.

It's only by trying to get it all right
that I see the futility plaguing my mind.
I'll put it like this: some people see faith
as a choice that needs energy in order to sustain.
So long as I've lived, that isn't the case —
faith is the friend that gives me a break.
All the above would have killed me before
I made it this far, were it not for the Lord.

I get why the world is put off by Christ.
But I get they forget there's free will within life.
I get why the people stay away from the steeple,
But I get they forget that we might as well try.

Faith saved my life. That's easy to say,
because faith is the basis for every day.
I wake in the morning. I eagerly pray:
thank you, my God, for giving me faith.

I took a turn to write a lyric,
And pretty soon I couldn't hear it.
I became a boy in bed who's going to fight
The boogeyman with his flashlight.

And as soon as I saw this,
As soon as it clicked,
I put down the flashlight
And ruined the trick.

"I'm doing too much,"
I said to myself,
"Pursuing profundity
in horrible health."

A stuttering sycophant,
Sick to the bone.
Several iterations
Before it hits home.

Sometimes it's best to let good be good.
Faith and grace go hand in hand.
You have the latter, now look to the first.
The wise proceed where they can't understand.

Wordy

We've got steeples of peoples
with peepholes in regions
of legions of demons and devils.
The level of seasonal
tea on my tongue
is determined by bumping
big boots on a bum
all like giddy-up go
in a girly igloo
with a compass containing
a gallon of glue.
The level of reason
is determined by treason.
It's determined by what?
It's determined by treason.
The fees of the feasible
eat what is edible,
read what is credible,
greet the regrettable,
feed the Gepettos of
puppets and puppies
and puggles and muggles
and mutants and marvels
and Stan Lee and Bruce Lee
and Jet Li and jet planes
and Plain Janes and Jane Does
and dos tres and hey, look,
I get it, it's lickety splicket.
I jumped over that fence
and it was a picket.
Admit it, I did it,
I made this exhibit.
If you can't speak truth,
I ask you to zip it.
Flick it, it's fun.
Dip it, it's dumb.
Decadent truth.

Tick it, it's
Tum, Tum-Tum-Tum, TUMS®!
With it I wish it would
mimic. It won't. It will
trickle, icicle, a nickel
it wants. Listen, don't leave.
Fickle my knees.
High time for tea,
if you ask me.
Sit it a minute
to teach it to tango to
edit and mangle my
lyrical geeeeeen-ius, it's a bus.
Yes, it's a bus. Out of my way,
cause here comes a bus.
I saved a baby
that almost got hit.
I am a hero.
I am legit.
Should I be flippant
within my exhibit?
It is my exhibit.
Flippant's my privilege.
Cartilage ear,
and cartilage nose.
But what's in my skull?
Nobody knows.
Listen, don't leave.
Fickle my sleeves.
Shiver me timbers
and breathtaking breeze.
Abusive, intrusive,
how rude is the moose who is
asking for jam to
go with his muffin.
Give that moose nothin.
Be done with the day.
Et tu Brute?

Shake yo boo-tay.
Motion's a potion
that poison's your bones
with an oxymoron
called progressive recession.
The test is in guessing
when's best to confess that
your best is still less than
a man in a city
who is like, "Honey, let's go
to that Broadway show,"
and she's like, "Yes, that sounds lovely.
So perfectly lovely."
And they go and they wine
and they dine and they find
that their life is so lovely.
So perfectly lovely.
But they have no time
to write out these lines.
No they have no time
to write out these lines.
No, they have no time
to write out these lines.
I bring the verbals
to revitalize,
to energatize,
to ostra-muh-size,
to straight up baptize,
to swat at some flies,
to bake me some pies.
Speed it up, slowly.
Break the routine
of rhythm and meter.
Goodbye, Aunt Serene.
Take a breath to buy some time.
. . .
Such a convenient line.

Alright, you ready?
Now ready looks like reedy
and I'm getting rather needy,
but reading a book is like
breaking your neck when
you're terribly tired of
witnessing witnesses
witness a witness
who's witnessing witnesses
witness a witness
who's witnessing
a miscellany at best.
Lest thou wishes magic fishes
taking turns and placing bets
on some sick aquatic version
of Russian roulette.
Ugh. You make me sick.
Now never say again
there is no token a la mode,
cause if I'm being fully honest
I'm all ready, set, and go,
just like I'm falling from a building
because I'm kissing vertigo.
Or like I'm writing to pretend
that I am Edgar Allen Poe.

See, I make my keep
in a deep sheep sleep
with a heap of a helping
of Hamburger Helper,
because when they were married,
they could only afford
some Hamburger Helper,
and not a lot more,
and all they could do
was pray for the two
they hoped to conceive.
Then one day they moved
far from their friends

with the two that they had —
my two older brothers.
My mom and my dad.
And then they had me,
their bundle of weird.
Surprise to my parents,
but God wanted me here.
And given the living
conditions I entered,
I hardly considered
my life to be sinister.
Mom was a teacher.
Dad was a minister.
Hard to deny it,
my life as a Southerner.
Simpler, for certain,
the lessons I learned
they were not on the surface
but burned like a furnace
beneath all my senses
and deep in my heart
and they taught me I ought to be
thoughtfully part
of the art all around me.
Engaged in reality,
embracing morality
and spirituality.
Enraged by evil thought
and counting it all
as magnificent loss
if I neglected the lesson
of loving my God.
I had my toys, but truth be told,
my favorite kind of play
was as an artisan refining
everything I had to say.
What joy I found within the sounds
of what a person said.

My toys were silly syllables
secreting from my head.

Like flapjack pancake paddled the rake.
Tiptoe panda bear made a mistake.
Hip hop hooligan taking a break.
Now break me off a piece of that Kit Kat cake.

You see, every little usage
of some sick alliteration
has the powerful potential
to expedite the expiation
of existence for a person
who sees existence in summation
as futility belittling
the human situation.
The creation of verbiage
becomes mundane and worthless
when we degrade human beings
and then say we can see
the way words pack a punch,
and at that we're a bunch
of belittling babies,
creating the makeup
of the existence we're hating.
Forsaking our faith
in the hope for a future
that features humanity
improving its use
of the beautiful tool
we have labeled as language.

Now ain't it a shame to treat words this way,
like their significance is different with every new day?
They serve as the substance for the thoughts that we say.
They promote the deep hope in the prayers that we pray.
They accuse and destroy as the hate we display.
And when their existence dissolves, their sentiments stay.

Woof.

But, what better toy than the word on the tongue,
whose maker created it simply for fun?
What better joy than the sound of the strum
from the tongue that is ticking and tocking out puns?
What other boy gets a gun like this one,
a weapon whose conception is the blessing of God?
And what better closer for a composer so dumb
than a gesture expressed without words in a nod.

Undertaker

I tend to write poems within a rhythm-rhyme fashion
To discover potential while making love to my passion,
This language I practice to tell the weak to take action
To make a way for themselves in a world where they have no traction.

I milk this cow I call English for every drop that she's got
To take a bucket of verbiage into the stream of my thought.
I have no fear of brittle bones being broke by insecure hate,
Creating for the sake of making great from the naught.

What's naught is a sentence that hinges on deprivation
Of a human's capability to find motivation.
I find it sick and absurd to use the power of word
To knock a man down in the midst of his tribulation.

And that's an introduction to the problem we face —
Hatred using its language to take a stab at God's grace.
So I milk this cow daily to find some wisdom-filled ways
To verbally remove these undertakers from their place.

It's not political or critical, it's simply analytical
To say that being cynical is literal death.
Have we tried it? Yes, we know when we contrive it and go
We murder the soul of the hopeful with our cynical breath.

What is further, when we murmur verbal murder we begin
To bury the burden born by our beautiful sin,
Which we committed then admitted, "Sure, we'd do it again,"
Because we're high on adrenalin from abusing our friends.

How empowering this glowering tone in our voice
That has us showering venom with our articulated noise.
We use some flowery words to trick the little girls and boys,
But our method is hollow. It is the cowardly choice.

Don't miss my meaning, lean in closer to hear it —
I do not hate who we are; I hate our cowardly spirit.
It is a product of automatic robotic behavior.
Without interruption we go on hating our neighbor.

So I'm using my verbiage to be my method to how
I might break this behavior — it is an interrupting cow.
This cow I call English, it's just a gift from the light
To verbally murder my undertaker inside.

Under My Eyelids

The eager eyes I feast with daily
Have now found blessed retreat.
And yet my mind takes on the cause
Of standing up to sleep.
My mind reminds my other half
I'm withered and I'm weak
To pose ironic argument
That I'm not fit for sleep.
A silly game, my mind does play,
Whose goal looks like defeat.
Its gameplay is perpetual,
Its players cannot sleep.
It's silly how it operates,
Determined to repeat.
I ask for mercy but my mind
Neglects my plea to sleep.
Alas, I leave my mind to fret,
Such stress I do not need.
I join my eyes beneath the shades
That try to trap the sleep.
But once I'm here, I wonder how
This trial came to be.
I've done no crime and still my mind
Indicts my right to sleep.
Such anger rises toward my mind.
It drips of lunacy.
I've half a mind to curse myself
And half to fall asleep.
But my intentions have no say.
My will is far too weak.
My mind is rogue and all I know is
It won't let me sleep.
I set myself to self-destruct.
I am the enemy.
If I destroy the villain,
I will rescue precious sleep.
How do I undermine my mind?

It's hard to say the least.
But if I drain its energy,
Then I will have my sleep.
Out of bed, lights turned on,
With pencil and a sheet,
I start a poem knowing this
Will be my path to sleep.
I make my verse repetitive,
My way of counting sheep.
I make my foe my sedative,
My way of catching sleep.
I write until I feel my mind
Ease its grip on me.
And then I write my final line.
It's time to go to sleep.

Words

Words are very funny things.
They are creatures you create.
You can use them to improve the world
or curse the world with hate.

Words are what you use to say
"I love you" to your mother.
They're the monsters that you might let loose
when angry at another.

Your words can feel less powerful
than what they really are,
But words contain the power
to transform a person's heart.

You speak a thought composed of words
for someone else to hear,
And, depending on those words,
you push them far or draw them near.

Words are just the end result
of a choice you make inside —
A choice to let a thought run free
or force that thought to hide.

It's important that you understand
the way words shape this life,
Because the words you use are how you choose
your views on wrong and right.

If you forget that words have power,
do not be surprised
When a word you speak to one you love
leaves tears within their eyes.

If you forget that words are creatures,
beware that once they're said,
You cannot get them back,
for they've escaped out of your head.

Words have grand potential,
yet some speak with such despair,
Callous or oblivious
To how they rot the air.

Life is like a big ole ship,
and words are like the rudder —
We set our destinations
with each syllable we utter.

You might choose an angry word
to match the flame within.
Such choices might direct your course
to losing precious friends.

You might choose a thought-filled word
to make more thoughts transpire.
Such words have been the tiny sparks
that set the world on fire.

Or you may choose the word that's good
to heal a damaged soul.
Sometimes the heart is hungry
and that word can make it full.

Don't use your words too quickly,
for you've only got a few
Before the people hear your words
and understand how you are you.

That's not to say you ought to live
in fear of what they think —
It's merely wise to check your words
before you go to speak.

That's not to say you ought display
a person you are not —
It's simply in your interest
to best articulate your thoughts.

I heard two words when I was young
that made me reconsider
The value had in staying mad
or choosing to be bitter.

Those words I heard seemed so absurd,
and yet I came to find
Those words and all the things that brought me joy
were quite aligned.

So I use those words each morning
when I get up out of bed
To fight away the yucky thoughts
that creep into my head.

Some days it isn't easy
to feel these words inside,
But I say them all the same
because I love my silly life.

The next time you feel down or angry,
give these words a try —
Take three deep breaths and then say, "Thank you!"
while looking at the sky.

For "thank" and "you" are powerful
when paired up as a team.
Just say them once a day
and you will find out what I mean.

I heard three words when I was small,
And I heard them very often.
I was unaware, but over time
They caused my heart to soften.

Later on, in retrospect,
I understood their force.
Knowing that another loves you
Can redirect your course.

So I used these words, not flippantly,
But when I felt them true.
I wanted to bless the ones I loved
With "I" and "love" and "you".

Just these few words throughout my life
Have changed the way I am.
I am convinced the grace of God
Is how these words began.

Words are very funny things.
You get to choose your own.
They're the choices that determine
Whether or not you are alone.

So make the choices good ones
When there's something you must tell.
I thank you and I love you.
These words have served me well.

GOOD FIGHT, GOOD NIGHT

A Call to Good

Good Fight

There are good fights and there are bad fights,
And we should not be mistaken on this point.
Some exist to end pain and plight.
Others arise from pedantic pride.
Before you know if your fight is good,
You must select a side and join.
Otherwise, what meaning resides in a notion like "should"?
If you have not consciously and previously committed to a side,
Then do not fight.
If you cannot help yourself, then fight in the faith that your fight is good,
But know that your faith is blind,
And hope your zeal does not destroy that which is good and kind.

Terrence Bo, the Baker's Goat

Terrence Bo, the Baker's Goat,
Watched the Baker come and go.
Morning sun on the trees,
Terrence Bo would watch him leave.
Reddish sky, evening sun,
Terrence Bo would watch him come.
"Evening, Bo," the Baker said.
He'd hand the goat some stale bread.

Terrence Bo loved the bread.
He'd chew it up and bob his head.
The Baker then would go inside
And greet and kiss his lovely Wife.

Terrence Bo loved the Wife.
She kept a garden right outside,
And in the garden, in sunlight,
She'd sit by Terrence Bo and write.
Pulling carrots from the ground,
Writing to the crunching sound.
Eating carrots by the Wife,
Standing still, loving life.

Terrence Bo loved the life.
Couldn't read, though he tried.
Bless the Wife — she would recite
Stories of courageous knights.

Terrence Bo loved those guys.
Saving damsels caught in plight.
Terrence Bo stood so tense,
Chewing carrots in suspense.
Hero battles evil wizard.
Goat emotions in a blizzard.
Hero triumphs in the end.
Bleating happy as a kid.
Wife pets Terrence Bo to say,
"Thank you, Bo, you've made my day."

Terrence Bo loved the life.
Terrence Bo loved the Wife.
Terrence Bo loved the bread.
A happy goat, loved and fed.

Until the day the Mayor's Son
Went out looking for some fun.
Strapping man, could charm a flea.
Pretty hair and pretty teeth.
Such satisfaction in himself.
Festooned in his father's wealth.
He could afford to work for free.
He called his work philosophy.
Though most would dub his occupation
Flattery, inebriation.
Out of bed by nine or ten,
To the bar for morning gin.
Leave the bar 'round one or two.
Stroll the street with naught to do.

He often went to get some bread,
His belly wet yet not yet fed.
The Baker always took the toll.
The Mayor's Son in drunken droll.
Pretty boy with bread in hand.
Righteous words, underhand.

The Baker doesn't judge the man.
Lets him spew, no reprimand.
He asks the Mayor's Son a question.
Philosophaster provides a lesson.
The Baker sees it's just no use.
This man does dialogue abuse —
The Baker sets up dialogue.
It's commandeered for monologue.

The Mayor's Son would down the bread
Then touch his chin and tilt his head.
"Delicious bread. Perhaps consider
Harder crust and softer center."

He'd then extend a breath to savor
The moment he had done a favor,
Then reach out with a tactful measure,
"Thank you, sir, it's been a pleasure."

Typically, the Mayor's Son
Returned for early evening rum.
He'd down a few then stand up proud
To greet the weary working crowd.
"Evening, comrades!" Arms stretched high.
"The day is done," he'd say with sigh.
The folks would order pints of beer.
He'd cheers his rum and sing, "Here, here!"

The Mayor's Son pretended he
Renounced his privileged pedigree
To spend these hours with the folks
Who saw right through his haughty hoax.
"Long day for me," between his sips.
Shaking head and pursing lips.
"I do my best to make my rounds,
To give some cheer back to this town."
Exaggerated exhalation.
"Difficult, keeping patient.
Just wish more folks would choose to see
The joy within philosophy."
Shaking head, forlorn sighs.
Gathered crowd rolling eyes.
Spewing such throughout the eve,
The Mayor's Son, the last to leave.
Stumble home, fall, asleep.
Up by ten o'clock. Repeat.

One day when leaving morning gin,
The Mayor's Son, upon a whim,
Did not go to the Baker's shop,
But to the woods to take a walk.
He wanted something fun to do,
And, if not fun, the woods were new,

And before long, stopped in his tracks,
"What is this?" he softly asked.
A clearing in the woods in which
A cottage sat, a picket fence,
A garden. But what caught his eye,
Radiant damsel. Goat beside.

Smoothed his hair and cleared his throat.
Gaiting toward the girl and goat.
Startled woman. Apologies.
Flattering soliloquys.
Terrence Bo, chewing carrots,
Listening in decent spirits.
Mayor's Son shoos goat away.
Sits down in Bo's favorite place.
Terrence Bo, now disconnected,
Watches, angry and rejected.

The Mayor's Son immodestly
Strokes the woman's hair, but she
Swats his hand, stands to her feet.
"I think it's best for you to leave."

He stands and tries his words again.
She is not interested in him.
She turns to go, he grabs her arm.
On the ground, full-blown alarm.
On top of her, he holds her down,
Caressing edges of her gown.
She struggles but cannot escape,
Crying out her dreadful fate.

Goat emotions in a blizzard.
"Must defeat this evil wizard."
Striking hoof into the dirt,
Lowers head but still alert.
Taking aim, starting charge,
Target growing ever large.

The Mayor's Son lifts his gaze,
Takes a goat head to the face.
Laid out cold, broken nose,
Two black eyes. The work of Bo.

The woman does not hesitate.
To her feet then runs away.

The Mayor's Son there on the ground,
Motionless and not a sound.
Terrence Bo just watches him.
If needed, Bo will charge again.

The Mayor's Son opens eyes,
Sits up straight and then he finds
A group of folks standing round,
Staring at him on the ground.
The goat, the Wife, and the Baker,
Two constables beside the Mayor.
The Mayor sighs. "My son, alas,
Why must you be such an ass?
Thank God this goat has got more sense.
His head is hard, but you are dense."

They took the Mayor's Son away
And locked him up that very day.
It took time for the Baker's Wife
To recover from her shock and fright.
It never fully went away,
But when she did think of that day,
She knew that, in the midst of fear,
Something good was also there.
The Wife thanked God for Terrence Bo,
Hero, friend, guardian goat.

Quiet

I live in a silent world where noise does not exist
There are no sounds of footsteps coming
There are no beats from fingers drumming
There is no shatter when glass is broken
Words are written and never spoken
The world agreed long ago
To do away with audio
When words had lost significance
And music bred indifference
And now we live in silent modes
Smiling everywhere we go
Passing friends and shaking hands
Profoundly quick to understand
That this whole world was made to be
A stage to show humanity
An ironic twist in which the stars
Are the audience, and here we are
Acting out this grand production
Showing, now, with noise reduction
And the reviews are in, the critics rave
It's as if we're watching a different play
At first, you fear, a silent film
Might leave you bored and unfulfilled
But keep on watching, notice how
The actors pay attention now
They see the bits they once had missed
And find it fun to reminisce
On simple things like food and drink
And with the silence they can think
Deeper, longer, better, more
They now understand the world
This never was a place of fear
Not until we brought it here
This globe that hosts humanity
Now turns itself in irony
For once it boasted lovely sound
But gluttony ran it to the ground

Music turned to bitter noise
And we were left without a choice
We banished sound, now silence covers
All the lips of all these lovers
And now we live this irony
Maintaining silent harmony
Passing friends and shaking hands
Profoundly quick to understand
I live in a silent world where noise does not exist

An Introvert Among Wolves

Nigel needed nearly every moment he could get
In which the world allowed him air to breathe and space to simply sit.
Perhaps he would have found his fill if the world did not condemn
The practices of introverts that come from needs within.

In meetings Nigel found himself tracking conversation,
Taking in the back and forth in stern deliberation.
He aimed to give due diligence to the information.
But his coworkers would meet this aim with clear disapprobation.

"Nigel," Curtis always said, "stop holding back your thoughts."
Though he knew it was no use, Nigel would respond, "I'm not."
"Nigel," Jen would then explain, "this is a thinking pot.
We're making stew from all the thought ingredients we've got."

"And if you don't contribute," Deb would pick it up from there,
"Well I guess it's just a question as to why you're even here."
"Now let's not be too hasty," Tom would say, "that's not quite fair.
Nigel pulls his weight and we all know that's very clear."

"But he doesn't speak his mind," Scott liked to keep the feud alive.
Nigel then would take a breath to speak, but Scott would simply sigh,
"Nigel just sits back, and I've begun to wonder why
He's even in these meetings." Scott would give the evil eye.

Nigel then would just begin to posit a retort
Before Tom would jump back in again, Nigel left ignored.
His colleagues would go back and forth 'til Ally cut them short,
"Let's table this for later and get back to the report."

Nigel left the meetings between anger and disgust,
A victim of the symptoms of the extraverted fuss.
They never would resolve the matter, and that was just because
It's nice to have a whipping boy. And that's what Nigel was.

The First to Rot

The first time is always the hardest,
Saying you believe in God.
It's hard because you're worried you might never say it again,
And then you'll have made yourself a fool for saying it.
Granted, I've only said it for the first time once.
But I know it's the hardest,
If it's sincere.
The implications you invite into your life with such a statement
Stultify your very existence up to that point,
And that is frightening.
But whether or not you embrace these implications,
There is no less foolishness in your existence.

What have you prayed to God for?
That's a valid question for me to ask,
For if I am in some way curious about you,
Curious enough to ask you a question,
What better curiosity to have
Than that for your soul's desire?

If you believe in God, do you have to believe in the existence
Of the soul?
Is it possible that there is God, up there and around and stuff,
And we are soulless beings,
Operating on a physiology, a substance monist reality
Where our thoughts and emotions are physicality byproducts?

What happens if there is God,
Up there and around and stuff,
And somebody gets to meet him and asks him a question like,
"Why'd you put my soul in that body?"
And he says something like,
"Your soul is that body."
What then?

What then? What then? Oh friend, my friend.
I've said it before, and I'll say it again,
The first time's the hardest to believe there is sin.

91

Because you tried it. Delighted, you did it again.
And now you're admitting you're an imperfect ten —
Another God, an idol, vain usage, and then
No Sabbath, no honor, you murder your friend,
Adultery and theft, the lies you extend,
Top it off with our envy, that's ten out of ten.

So bleak, this sneak peak of what's beneath our smiling teeth.
We are infested with a substance come from actions
Invested in the pursuit of selfish cravings.
But each of us picks when we want to admit it.
The first time is always the hardest,
Saying you believe in God,
Not because it's hard to believe in God,
But because it's hard to believe in ourselves,
What we've done,
The things we've granted our smiling approbation.

There's reason to this rhyme,
A season to this time,
An open window that might be a squeeze to pass through,
But it leads to truth.

Don't give up on saying you believe in God for the first time,
And make every time your first time,
With the gasping profundity of recognizing the error of your ways
So that you may be set on course,
Washed by the blood of the Lamb
Who was killed by his own love,
His love for a people who cannot decide whether or not they want to love fully.
Quit playing this game with yourself
Over how much you're willing to submit.
Be done with it either way and walk straight into the horizon of your choice.
Because a heart standing still is the first to rot.

The Wise Pause

He took a beating for believing there were demons who demeaned him.
We could see the way he suffered. He said Satan was his brother.
When we listened to his reasons we could tell that he believed them.
The Bible was his basis, but he said the book's archaic.
Not to mention why he wanted our attention to begin with —
He was sitting on the stoop of the apartment that we live in.
When we walked up, he looked at us, then he whispered, "Don't go in."
When we told him that we lived there, he just whispered it again.

So we asked him why we shouldn't, he said, "Sometimes faith is needed."
We said, "Reason has a purpose," then he finally conceded.
"I'll provide an explanation. It requires you be patient.
I will try to expedite it, but you've got to pay attention."
We agreed that we would listen. He said, "Sit down on the stoop."
We got seated. He proceeded with a story he claimed true.

"There is a God." That's how he started, and we nodded. We agreed.
"And God is one." He shivered at the wind. We told the man, "Indeed."

He said, "Are you familiar with the prodigal son's story?"
We nodded, and we asked his name. He told us it was Mory.
"I'm glad you know the parable, that saves us quite some time.
I'll move right to the point to get right to the bottom line.
What would you say if I told you the true prodigal son
Was Lucifer, who walked away, who's since been on the run?"

We took a moment just to process what this question meant to say.
Then we asked him, "Are you saying God wants Satan back one day?"

"Think about it," Mory told us. "Think of what you know of God.
All-loving and forgiving, right?" We couldn't help but nod.
"And the son within that parable abandons what he knows.
He leaves but then returns and, well, you know how this one goes.
So what if Satan's currently pursuing his desire,
Squandering his wealth while setting human souls on fire?
And what if, when he's finished, he decides he ought return,
Hoping God will take him back and bridges aren't yet burned?"

What weight within these questions — we could not help but pause.
We felt we should dismiss them, but did we have just cause?
Extreme, it seemed, this pondering upon his proposition.
Lesser theories have invoked malicious opposition.
And yet, something about it, the way it left his lips,
As if this wasn't theory, but a memory of his.
We thought another moment then we asked a simple question,
"If what you say is true, then what's the purpose of this lesson?"

Mory giggled while he sat there on our stoop and then he said,
"The purpose is to realign the thoughts within your head.
You hold a set of thoughts as truth, but with new information,
Your understanding may transform based on new interpretation."

We'd heard this sort of spiel before, framework without flesh.
"What's the bottom line here? Tell us plain without finesse."

Mory giggled once again, a giddy-looking bloke.
He finally stood to his feet, wiped his butt and spoke.
"Christians think of Satan as the enemy, all the while
The Bible says to love your enemy." He ended with a smile.

When standing up, we registered that Mory was quite tall.
The words he spoke had intrigue, but they lacked a wherewithal.

"If that is God's intention, would not the Bible simply say it?"
Mory rolled his eyes. "That book is cryptic and archaic."

We did not like his tone for it implied his true intention,
But we wanted a real answer, not this cheap way of dismissing.

"Why would this be the first we've heard, if this was truly true?
Would not a theory such as this have come long before you?"

"What difference does it make?" Mory answered without pause.
At that point we were thoroughly exhausted by his cause.

"We can see your plot is hollow and you have no real desire
To have real conversation, and we suspect you are a liar.
There is something kind of fishy here, we tried to hear you out,
But when we asked for education you betrayed what you're about.

Your intentions look to be no more than giving glitzy thought
To distract your sucker audience from focusing on God.
See your theory may have traction but you haven't a good reason
For your audience to buy in. Ultimately, it's a tease and
The son who left his father had to choose it for himself.
He went back to his father after squandering his wealth.
So if that's what Satan wants to do, then let him make his choice.
We've made it for ourselves, so relieve us of this noise.
Now we are tired of your spewing, we just wish to go to bed."
As we spoke these words we watched as Mory's skin tone turned to red.

Yep, you guessed it, sure enough, this guy Mory was a demon.
And he lost his cool all because we chose not to believe him.

"I tried to do the easy way," he told us in a huff,
"By converting you, but looks like that was simply not enough.
There are demons I report to, and I will not be their joke.
Now I will end you," he announced while exhaling puffs of smoke.

Sprouting horns, growing tall, and then baring vicious claws,
Before I tell you more, I feel that I must pause.

You may have wondered who else has been present here with me.
After all, I have been candid in the pronoun choice of "we".
There's a simple explanation, but first you ought to hear
That if you choose to read this further, it gets a little weird.

There's an itty-bitty angel who is strapped to my back
With an itty-bitty tommy gun he holds in his hands.
And wherever I go, this angel's my man.
He keeps me safe from demons and their wily sneak attacks.
The demons tell my angel, "We're just chilling here, bro."
Says my angel, "I believe you, but my tommy gun don't."[1]

See Mory was a special case. I guess I'd had enough.
I saw him for his nature and I called him on his bluff.
So he had the upper hand when he delivered the first blow.
I slammed into the concrete. Said my angel, "Goodness, no."

1. *Home Alone 2: Lost in New York,* film, directed by Chris Columbus (1992; Chicago, IL: Twentieth Century Fox, Hughes Entertainment).

He jumped off my back, and he stood there with a grin.
With his gun pointed at Mory, "Say hello to my little friend."[2]
He lit that demon up. That demon didn't have a chance,
Mory getting shot in a pop, lock, and drop-it dance.

When Mory hit the ground, his form withered down to ash.
My itty-bitty angel stopped his firing at last.
He looked at me and I could see concern for my wellbeing.
"I'm fine," I told him casually, "I can take a beating."

My itty-bitty angel leaned his gun upon his shoulder.
Relieved but still he teased, "Man, you know you're getting older."

"Whatever," I responded. "I could've taken him, you know."
"I believe you," said my angel. "But my tommy gun don't."[3]

We went inside still laughing at how he kept his catchphrase fresh.
I paused to say, "I love you, man." My angel is the best.

2. *Scarface,* film, directed by Brian De Palma (1983; Key Biscayne, FL: Universal Pictures).

3. *Home Alone 2: Lost in New York.*

Monks and Ogres

Lyricist ogres boast on the ways
They've taken advantage of corporeal grace.
Lyricist monks boast on what they can find
On expeditions confined in their mind.
Because the mind is theirs and it's all in their power
To seek after knowledge to find and devour,
To grow their mentality into an ocean
Whose waters can swallow the shallow commotion
Of those whose intentions are poisoned with hate.
Not hating them back, they stop the mistake.
Lyricist monks push boundaries further
By looking at nature and watching it nurture.
Most find this monastery piously weird.
But it's only a usage of fickle veneer
To deter the fruition of feelings within
That look to be good but only pretend.
Lyricist ogres are dangerous creatures,
Pestilent poison packed with pretty features.
The product is thought and it's easy to cheat
When they make it appealing by using a beat.
And the people consuming it know that it's wrong —
They don't agree but still put it on.
"It's music. It's poetry. Hell, it's just fun."
Swallow such nonsense. Kiss logic gone.
Those truly against the words of a song
Don't let it play and say that it's fun.
Consider a song that advocates slavery.
How fun must it be to alter its nature?
It's evil to treat it as fun in part.
No matter the rhythm, no place in the heart.
The lyricist ogres are laughing at us,
Winning their boast on our lack of disgust.
The lyricist monks devote their existence
To the expedition intent on resistance.
An ongoing quest. An epic unending.
Decide on a side and stop pretending.

Tad Montgomery

There's a puppy dog resident up on West 84
Who lives in the window of the little puppy store.
His name is Tad Montgomery, or Gomer for short.
His favorite food is dog food, but he really isn't sure.

Gomer spends his afternoons thinking hard in silence
Until his nap time rolls around and heavy are his eyelids.
Gomer dreams of cuddling, and deep inside he likes it,
But Gomer wakes a loner, and, if questioned, he denies it.

"Too tough a pup," he always claims, "to care for such a thing."
"Keep walking," Gomer says to all the people on the street.
"Besides, with an owner, I would have to wipe my feet
Every time I come inside, and that just isn't me."

And so, this Tad Montgomery repeats his every day
Insisting that the window is the place he wants to stay.
A girl comes to the glass to press her nose up to the pane.
His tail wags, he licks the glass, but then she walks away.

"Good riddance," Gomer calls. "I am so happy that we're through!
She really was a nuisance, and I've many things to do."
Gomer paces 'round his space a minute, maybe two.
"I'm glad she left — her humid breath was fogging up my view."

Sunset on the city shows a Gomer still upset.
"That dummy girl, so good she's gone," is all the puppy says.
The stars begin to twinkle, and he knows it's time for bed.
He goes to sleep with visions of the girl stuck in his head.

The next day passes, then the next, and soon it's been two weeks.
Gomer's getting bigger but his spirit's growing meek.
"Why don't people like me?" Gomer wonders at the street.
"Alone I wake. Alone I wait. Alone I go to sleep."

Every time a passerby stops to look inside,
Gomer is a little less excited and alive.
Until he hits the point where, when a boy gives it a try
To get the pup's attention, Gomer simply gives a sigh.

"Tap the glass all you please, I will not be your laugh,
Dancing like an idiot behind the prison glass.
I've come to see reality is bitter and, alas,
I'd rather know no life at all than suffer having half."

But the boy continues tapping until Gomer comes to find
That the boy is simply tuning out what's happening behind.
The parents of the little boy are lost within a fight.
Gomer sees the tears within the boy's unblinking eyes.

"Puppy duty calls." Gomer stands up to his feet.
He waddles to the window, and there he takes a seat.
He looks up at the boy, and once their gazes meet,
Gomer lifts a paw to say, "I think you're really neat."

The boy just gives a sniffle and wipes away a tear.
Gomer says, "I'm also sad. I wish I wasn't here."
And then in an attempt to give the boy a little cheer,
Gomer kicks with his back leg to scratch his floppy ear.

As the boy is watching, he sniffles once again,
But this time it is paired up with a chuckle and a grin.
Gomer feels the thrill of what it means to have a friend.
But then the boy is pulled away, and Gomer's feeling ends.

"No!" Gomer cries. He bellows out his soul.
He whines and tries to find a way to meet his desperate goal.
He throws a fit within his pit. He kicks his water bowl,
For he can't remember the last time his heart had felt so full.

That puppy dog stayed heated the remainder of the day.
The sky could sense his mind and turned a bitter shade of gray.
He watched the street unblinkingly with nothing more to say.
His face stayed dry with anger while the window cried with rain.

The gray turned into black, and the moon could not be found.
The hours passed along. Gomer didn't make a sound.
And just before the dawn, Gomer finally laid down.
"I'm done," he whispered to himself. "Just put me in the ground."

Some stories have a happy ending. Others simply don't.
The happy ones we scoff at and consider them a joke.
We are calloused because sadness is the ending that we know.
Like Gomer, we are loners. We have given up on hope.

But Gomer woke to tiny fingers playing with his ears.
The groggy puppy yawned and saw his boy was standing there.
Not sure why he returned, Gomer really didn't care.
In the past he had been burned, yet now his hope began to flare.

Gomer had a history, but when it came to this,
Gomer chose to hope once more instead of reminisce.
He wagged his tail for the boy. The boy gave him a kiss.
"This is the best day of my life," Gomer said in utter bliss.

By the time the boy was done, Gomer's heart was free.
For the moment he forgot about his recent misery.
And when the child spoke, the puppy nearly peed.
"Nice to meet you, Gomer. You're coming home with me."

Once there was a puppy dog who lived on 84
As a loner in the window of the little puppy store.
He was angry at his life. He was bitter at the world.
Then Gomer got a home and was a loner for no more.

Good 'n Bad

The beauty and the beast
are the east and the west,
the best and the least,
and, to a degree,
the exact same thing.

If you consider these pairs
to the point of their core,
you begin to comprehend
why less is more,
and you begin to comprehend
that the point of the world
will never touch
the way of the world.

Consider the kiss,
the hysteria within
the momentary lips upon lips
and the significance
of such a seemingly mundane display
of blibbering blabbering blubber
being put upon an opposing pair of flesh flappers
with the accepted exchange
of spittle for the little piece of perfect
that a pleasing kiss can give.

Now if the beauty is the east and the best
and the beast is the west and the least,
consider how the kiss
becomes a way to translate these.
The least appealing thing to me
while considering hypothetically
the act of using my lips to clean
the surface of any given thing
is a surface which continuously
is lathered with a liquid debris
secreted by an organic thing.
And yet we find we are without need

of a justification for doing the deed
of kissing the lips of a human being.
And in so doing we obliviously
meet our curious capability
of actively performing the feat
of crafting the beauty out of the beast.

The point I'm making with the kiss
is, because of the potential for romantic bliss,
we tend to choose to be remiss
in dwelling on the specific bits
that are kind of gross yet nonetheless
serve as the flesh to manifest
a fruition providing spiritual rest
to our yearnings resulting from loneliness.

And so it works in this ironic way,
in which the least dignified type of display
becomes the best because it culminates
into this "magic-moment, seize-the-day,
on-top-of-the-world" spiritual state.
It created the best out of the least
when it went so far west, it ended up in the east.
That's the beauty of the beast,
like the rib that was plucked from Adam,
out of the least came Eve.

Dichotomies are interesting.
Hot and cold, black and white,
up and down, wrong and right,
dichotomies are interesting.
They're little teams that shed some light
on what it means to have a life.
Initially it isn't clear
the way dichotomies interfere
with what would otherwise be chaotic.
But dichotomies can murder darkness.
Without dichotomies, where would we be?
Absolutes are not chains, but the chance to be free.

But stigmas and stenches have us singing this song —
we'll forget wrong and right if it shuns what is wrong.

Bathwater gone,
Now where is the baby?
Righteous or wrong?
No need. We have maybe.

I believe in moral absolutes,
that there is God, and he lets us choose.
And all the beautiful dichotomies in life
are hinting at this truth.
Righteous silence might seem hidden,
but the point of the noise
is to point us to the point
that we've been given a choice.
Some argue there is too much evil
to believe in a God who is good.
If God exists, any decent person
would and should assassinate him if they could.

Have they taken their thinking far enough?
Is there evil or is there not?
If not, then where do we get off
telling anyone to stop?
If so, then what is it?
And where is it from?
Was it a product of choice
when it first begun?

Regardless our beliefs,
we all serve the same sentence,
forced to reconcile evil
while maintaining existence.
I've heard a theory,
and it's the best one I know.
It claims evil is real
And God let it be so.
He created creatures
And let them decide

What choices to make
And how to live life.
But first he made clear
How best to live life,
What choices to make,
What's best to decide.
Then he let them be free
To do as they would.
The first bad choice
Was blurring what's good.

As more bad choices infested the mind,
What's good and what's bad became harder to find.
As more bad choices infested creation,
Life got worse for each generation.

And when so far west, it's an easier feat
To just say that you're not than to travel back east.
If the world were flat, it'd simply be best
To say you're nowhere when you know you're out west.

But Jesus made loopholes, and humans have found
That evidence suggests that the Earth is quite round.
Sail the sea and drop the illusion
Of moral absolutes equating delusion.

For faith is the shovel for digging up grace,
And grace is a mirror held up to your face.
And once you acknowledge he's beauty, you're beast,
You've gone so far west that you're now in the east.

The Book of the God of Fire

In the middle of the garden stood two trees,
One of life, with healing leaves,
The other, knowledge, good and evil.
Dust to Adam. Bone to Eve.

"From any tree, you're free to eat,
Except the one. Just let it be.
Eat of it and you will die.
Aside from that, you're fully free."

We ate the fruit. You gave us grace.
You gave us clothes but closed the place.
The garden guarded by flaming sword,
Back and forth. The human race.

We wandered wicked, no good in man.
Flood, restart. You start your plan.
You start with one. Stars and sand.
You make Abram Abraham.

Carcasses, he cuts in two.
Birds of prey, he shoos away.
A blazing torch appeared and passed
Between the pieces. That was you.

Isaac, Jacob, Joseph sold.
Joseph's life, remarkable.
Egypt, famine, family comes.
Jacob's blessing on his sons.

Passing time. Pharaoh's new.
No history. Joseph who?
Israelites multiplied.
Enslaved in Egypt. Where were you?

Four hundred years of brutal plight.
Slavery, infanticide.
Moses floats in basket boat
And grows and kills in broad daylight.

Moses flees and starts again.
Through burning bush you speak to him.
Plagues on Egypt. Exodus.
Wash away Egyptian sin.

Cloud by day and then, by night,
Pillar of fire to give them light.
Forty years of wandering.
Ten commandments. Wrong and right.

Your glory in consuming fire
Atop the tabernacle pyre.
Judges, kings, and giant slaying.
Perversion in the heart's desire.

Solomon prays, your fire comes down.
The Israelites worship, face to the ground.
Perversion in the heart's desire.
Exodus of living fire.

Prophets come and prophets go.
Elijah orchestrates a show.
He calls on you. Your fire falls.
You are God. You let them know.

Prophets come and prophets go.
Malachi to end the flow.
You promise Elijah before that day,
Then silence hits. No more to say.

Four hundred years. Familiar, no?
God, oh, God, where did you go?
No living God, but still religion.
No living flame, but still a show.

As centuries pass along,
Your people ache, moan, and long.
Where is the powerful promised Messiah?
God, oh, God, where have you gone?

The Jews' God goes missing. Rome quickly rises.
The Jews hope for warfare, not humble surprises.
But a god who is God puts our hoping to shame.
A girl has a baby, and this is the flame.

"Hark! The Herald Angels sing
Glory to the new-born King!
Peace on Earth, and Mercy mild
God and Sinners reconcil'd"[4]

The words of Malachi transpire —
A voice cries out of someone higher
Who will baptize with
The Holy Spirit and fire.

Jesus grows. At thirty, he
Begins his humble ministry.
He finds some blokes, spiritual jokes,
And tells these folks, "Come follow me."

He speaks of things like second birth
And bringing fire to the Earth.
Fulfilling prophecy left and right,
Ironic dichotomies are his work:

Compassionate correction. Humble might.
Promise to fill those who crave what is right.
Knocking religious. Befriending filth.
Feeding death the source of life.

Death be ruined by its food.
Posthumous vicissitude.
God is good? Debated question.
Resurrection offers proof.

The murdered body walks again,
Treading on the curse of sin.
Eats and talks and goes to heaven.
Two men say he'll come again.

4. "Hark! the Herald Angels Sing," Charles Wesley (1739), adaptation by George
Whitefield (1758).

On Pentecost, all together.
A violent wind. Indoor weather.
Each receives a fire tongue.
Behold, your Holy Spirit comes.

A massive movement. Martyrs die.
The fire spreads. No wonder why.
Torture men. They cannot lie.
They witnessed resurrected life.

Letters to churches help explain
How Jesus brought back living flame.
The law of the Jews, certainly strange
If not fulfilled with Jesus slain.

But in his death comes course correction
And hope springs forth from resurrection.
Claim the king who shattered shame
And he'll bestow the living flame.

John has vision of living water,
Flowing through the Tree of Life.
No more curse, and no more night.
Lamp not needed. You are light.

Good Night

There are good nights and there are bad nights,
And we do things to stack the odds,
Half-convinced we're the ones who decide.
The other half, the one we try to hide,
Knows a little something about reality,
Distinguishes pain from fatality.
For whatever reason and for so many reasons
We shy away from things within us,
Ideas and wisdoms we know would be helpful,
And we do this, just because . . .

How many neglected ideas and wisdoms
Have rotted away in the prison of a person,
Screaming to be let out as they watch things get worse?
And how many have yearned to see
A man let his prisoners go free,
While keeping their own inmates locked up?
You have the key to yourself
And not to anyone else,
And when you free the ideas and wisdoms
That you know will help,
That's a beautiful thing.

There is good and bad, I promise you,
And the choice of good comes in everything we do,
Even if it's just a simple thought,
How we hold onto that thought or let it go.
It gets confusing, I know,
But it's real.

And so there are good nights and bad nights,
And I say this because there are good fights and bad fights,
And at the end of the day, everything we've done and said
Informs the way in which we go to bed.

But that's only half of it, and not even truly half.
Because reality goes like this:
We can be messed up in our mind

And destroy that which is good and kind,
And see how we fit our own mold
Of criminal and despicable,
And we can hate ourselves and go to bed
Prisoners of our own heads,
And yet, there comes
The good morning, good morning,
Where the sun has been born,
And I don't know how, if you've felt those things before,
You can see the morning sun
And deny there is grace in the world.
It may not be completely clear,
But it is there.

If it's hazy and out of focus,
The corrective lens is resurrection.

We shy away from things within us
That we know would be helpful
For whatever reason and for so many reasons.
These reasons stand in the way.
God is good. Have faith.
And if he has placed something within you
That you know would be helpful
Because you know it is good,
Then let it go.
Perhaps it has a world to save.
Don't be the warden telling it "No".

The bad nights are bad nights
Because we keep our agony locked up,
Letting it feed on whatever remnants of good remain within.
While God waits with perfect patience
For you to give the agony to him.
It amounts to pain when we give it to God.
It becomes fatal when we do not.
Bad people can have good fights and good nights
By tapping into the source of life.
Jesus Christ. Mocked throughout time. He still takes the pain
For those who don't want it to be fatal. Have faith.

Good night, good night. Make it good, I pray,
By trusting in God to bring back the day.
Good night, good night. What more can I say?
Goodness will triumph in the end. Have faith.